Work & Play
Redwork Through the Day

Seriously cute! Irresistibly playful! Redwork embroidery designs by Lakadaisies are winning the hearts of stitchers everywhere with their folk-art portrayals of childhood. And now you can stitch ten of the whimsical designs from this one collection of patterns! *Work & Play—Redwork Through the Day* includes youngsters romping, playing games, and doing chores.

Each fun design uses only one or two easy embroidery stitches. And did you know? Redwork doesn't have to be red! Simply choose your favorite floss color to recreate these sweet children at work and play. Our complete instructions show you how to stitch the designs on cotton fabric and tea- or coffee-dye the completed stitched piece for an authentic folk-art look. Want your project to be a different size? On page 13, our formula tells you how to enlarge or reduce the designs.

When you're ready to celebrate the seasons with Lakadaisies redwork, visit LeisureArts.com and get your copy of Leisure Arts leaflet #5275, *Happiness & Cheer—Redwork Through the Year.*

designer DOLORES STORM

Dolores Storm and her husband John live near Lampasas, Texas, where they have a small shop. In the beginning, they sold antiques and quilts; then Dolores had the idea to sell her redwork embroidery stitched pieces.

"About twelve years ago," says Dolores, "I stitched some redwork designs for our gift shop. People loved them and wanted patterns they could stitch for themselves. So I said, 'Sure, I can do that,' and set about convincing John to help me create some patterns. We started with four designs that we also took to a local quilt shop. Now, thanks to the support of redwork fans everywhere, our Lakadaisies patterns are sold worldwide."

Dolores's interest in needlework began in her childhood. "I've always loved playing with fabric and thread," she says. "The way a simple line drawing can come to life with a few easy embroidery stitches is fascinating to me. In my opinion, simple stitches allow you to add more detail. And the more you add, the better it looks!"

To see the Storms' latest "Hand-Did Folk Art" patterns, visit Lakadaisies.com.

LEISURE ARTS, INC.
Little Rock, Arkansas

Gardening

Pattern on page 14.

Ironing

Pattern on page 15.

Pattern on page 16.

Wash A Dish

Pattern on page 17.

"This is the way we wash a dish"

Along Came A Spider

Pattern on page 18.

Pattern on page 19.

Jumping Rope

Pattern on page 20.

Driving

Pattern on page 21.

Rocking Baby

Pattern on page 22.

Skating

Pattern on page 23.

general instructions

SUPPLIES & TECHNIQUES

Fabric

Any light-colored, light- to medium-weight fabric is suitable for embroidery. These designs are stitched on 100% cotton unbleached muslin. Linen or flannel are also good choices.

Floss or Thread

There are many options for stitching. Six-strand cotton embroidery floss is widely available. Pearl cotton (size 8 and size 12) is another choice. A third option is Sulky® cotton thread, which is available in several weights.

Once your pattern is sized, work a sample, trying various numbers of floss strands, sizes of pearl cotton, or weights of thread.

Needles

Needles are a personal choice. A sharp point is necessary to pierce the fabric, but the size and type of the needle is up to you. Quilting betweens (size 8 or 10) are short, sharp needles, while embroidery needles (size 8 or 10) are longer. Try different size and style needles until you find one that suits you.

Hoop

It is important to keep the fabric stretched tightly while embroidering. Many stitchers prefer wooden hoops. A large hoop will allow you to work on most of the design before repositioning the fabric.

Other Tools

A needle threader comes in quite handy when using multiple strands of floss, while a needlecase safely stores your needles when not in use.

A thimble protects the middle finger while embroidering, but it can take some getting used to.

Small, sharp embroidery scissors clip thread and floss quickly and neatly. Protect the points (and your fingers!) by always storing the scissors in a leather sheath.

Sizing Patterns

Patterns may be sized to fit into standard size, ready-made frames. To change the size of a pattern, divide the desired height of the pattern by the actual height of the pattern. Multiply the result by 100 and photocopy the pattern at this percentage.

For example, you want to enlarge the pattern to $11\frac{1}{2}$" high and the pattern on the page is 10" high.
$$11\frac{1}{2} \div 10 = 1.15$$
$$1.15 \times 100 = 115\%$$
Copy the pattern at 115%

Or, to make the pattern smaller, say $7\frac{1}{2}$" high, use the same formula.
$$7\frac{1}{2} \div 10 = .75$$
$$.75 \times 100 = 75\%$$
Copy the pattern at 75%

Transferring the Design

The simplest method for transferring your design is to tape the fabric over the pattern on a sunny window; then, trace the design with a sharp #2 pencil or a fine-line water-soluble pen or marker. A glass top table with a lamp under it or a light box will work as well.

An alternative method uses Transfer-Eze™, a pliable film through which you can embroider. Just photocopy the sized design onto the "film" side of a Transfer-Eze sheet using the light setting on your jet printer. Remove the paper backing and adhere the pattern to the right side of the fabric. Embroider the design. Trim the excess Transfer-Eze film away from the embroidery. Soak the fabric in cold water to dissolve the remaining transfer film.

STITCHING INSTRUCTIONS

1. Size the pattern and cut two fabric pieces 3" larger on all sides than the pattern. Wash, dry, and press the fabric pieces (don't use fabric softener if you will be using Transfer-Eze™). Transfer the pattern to one fabric piece.
2. With right sides up and the transferred design on top, layer the fabric pieces and baste around the edges of the design.
3. Place the basted fabric pieces in the hoop, smoothing any wrinkles. It will be easier to embroider if the fabric is stretched tightly in the hoop.
4. Work Backstitches over all lines of the design, stitching through both layers of the fabric. Work French Knots for dots on the design. Use 2 strands of floss (or the heavier weight thread) for most of the stitching, switching to 1 strand (or the lighter weight thread) in the more detailed areas.
5. After all the embroidery is complete, hand wash the piece in a mild detergent and lay it flat to dry, smoothing any wrinkles as it dries. Place it design side down on a white or light-colored fluffy towel and press.
6. To add an antique look, soak the piece in weak tea or coffee. Once you get the color/mottling you want, rinse well and press the piece until it is dry.

The designer's models are stitched on muslin with color #1169 of Sulky® cotton thread in both 30 wt and 12 wt and are tea/coffee stained. Most of the patterns have been sized to fit ready-made 11" x 14" frames.

STITCHES
Backstitch
Backstitch is a simple embroidery stitch, comprised of short, even stitches that form an outline. Thread the needle with an 18" length of floss or thread and tie a small knot at one end. Bring the needle up through the fabric at 1 on a design line; go down into the fabric at 2. Come up through the fabric again at 3 *(Fig. 1)*. Continue to work in this manner, following the traced design lines *(Fig. 2)*. Each Backstitch will share a hole with the previous stitch and the next stitch. When going around tight curves, stitches should be closer together. To end your floss or thread, turn your work over and weave the floss or thread in and out of the completed stitches.

Fig. 1   **Fig. 2**

French Knot
French Knots are small knots that stand up from the fabric surface. Bring the needle up through the fabric at 1; wrap floss or thread around needle twice. Go down into fabric at 2, and holding floss or thread with the non-stitching fingers, tighten the knot as close to the fabric as possible, while pulling the needle through the fabric *(Fig. 3)*.

Fig. 3

1 2

Shown on page 2.

Shown on page 3.

Shown on page 4.

Shown on page 5.

"This is the way we wash a dish"

a woman's work is never done...

Shown on page 6.

Shown on page 7.

Shown on page 8.

Shown on page 9.

Shown on page 10.

Shown on page 11.

Credits

Instructional Writer: Mary Sullivan Hutcheson
Editorial Writer: Susan McManus Johnson
Graphic Artist: Angela Ormsby Stark

Leisure Arts, Inc., grants permission to the owner of this publication
to copy the patterns on pages 14-23 for personal use only.